Verleih uns Frieden

(Lord, in thy mercy grant us peace)

Words by Martin Luther (1483–1546)
English version by John Rutter

FELIX MENDELSSOHN (1809–47)
Edited by John Rutter

© Oxford University Press 1996. All rights reserved.

Printed in Great Britain

OXFORD UNIVERSITY PRESS MUSIC DEPARTMENT
GREAT CLARENDON STREET, OXFORD OX2 6DP • 198 MADISON AVENUE, NEW YORK, NY 10016
Photocopying this copyright material is ILLEGAL.

4

OXFORD

CHORAL
CLASSICS

Oxford Choral Classics Octavos

VERLEIH UNS FRIEDEN

FOR SATB CHOIR WITH ORGAN OR
ORCHESTRA

FELIX MENDELSSOHN

Edited by John Rutter

OXFORD UNIVERSITY PRESS

In 1830 Franz Hauser, a Viennese singer and Bach enthusiast, sent a Lutheran hymnal, the *Lutherisches Liedbüchlein,* to Mendelssohn, who was in Italy as part of his Grand Tour. This treasury of words and music inspired Mendelssohn to compose six chorale cantatas, two motets, and the present hymn-setting—which takes only Luther's text, the music being entirely Mendelssohn's own. He wrote to Hauser in January 1831: 'I intend to set the little song 'Verleih uns Frieden' as a canon with cello and bass', and by February the piece was complete. In the event, the canonic opening was for divided cellos, its theme both recalling the second subject from the *Hebrides* overture of 1830 and anticipating the opening clarinet motif from another overture, *Die schöne Melusine* (1833).

Source: Facsimile of autograph MS, in *AMZ* xli, supplement for June 1839. This gives the German text only. In the Rietz Collected Edition, the Latin text, *Da nobis pacem,* which was the source of Luther's hymn, is added. The organ reduction in the present edition is editorial.

JOHN RUTTER

The accompaniment is scored for 2 fl, 2 cl, 2 bsn, strings, and optional organ. Full orchestral scores and instrumental parts are available on rental from the publisher.

This piece is extracted from the Oxford Choral Classics anthology
European Sacred Music, edited by John Rutter.

Approximate duration: 4 minutes

Ver - leih uns_ Frie - den gnä - dig - lich, Herr Gott, zu un - sern_
Lord, in thy_ mer - cy grant__ us peace Through - out all ge - ne -

Zei - ten! Es ist doch ja kein_ An - drer nicht,
-ra - tions; Thou art a - lone our_ sword and shield,

ISBN 0 - 19 -341815 - 0